S0-BCY-533

CONTENTS

Recipes, text and trademarks ©2008 Riviana Foods Inc.

Photography on pages 3, 8, 9, 10, 12, 13, 14, 18, 19, 28, 33, 37, 44, 45, 47, 60, 62, 68, 69, 70, 72, 73, 74, 75, 83, and 94 © 2008 Riviana Foods Inc. All other photographs © 2008 Publications International, Ltd.

Minute® is a registered trademark of Riviana Foods Inc.

All rights reserved. This publication may not be reproduced or quoted in whole or in part by any means whatsoever without written permission from:

Louis Weber, CEO
Publications International, Ltd.
7373 North Cicero Avenue
Lincolnwood, IL 60712.

Permission is never granted for commercial purposes.

Manufactured in China.

ISBN-13: 978-1-4127-2701-3
ISBN-10: 1-4127-2701-4

Pictured on the front cover *(clockwise from top left)*: Easy Santa Fe Style Stuffed Peppers *(page 21)*, Easy Chicken and Rice Tacos *(page 78)*, Classic Minute Rice Pudding *(page 90)*, and Green Bean, Chicken and Rice Dinner *(page 30)*.

Pictured on the back cover *(clockwise from top left)*: Sesame Rice Salad *(page 5)*, Hoppin' John *(page 39)*, Apple Cinnamon Rice Crisp *(page 92)*, and Rice and Cranberry Pilaf *(page 66)*.

For consumer inquiries, please call 800-646-8831 (800-Minute1).

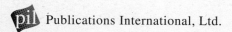 Publications International, Ltd.

STIR IT UP

Quick tips for adding complex carbohydrates to your daily diet.

Breakfast Scramble

Scramble eggs with hot cooked rice. Top with shredded cheese and pico de gallo or salsa.

Easy Fried Rice

Sautée minced garlic, shredded carrots, frozen green peas and diced cooked chicken or ham in cooking oil. Stir in cooked rice and soy sauce to taste.

Nutty Rice

To hot cooked rice, add peanuts, cashews, pine nuts or sunflower seeds. Stir in dried cranberries, cherries or blueberries for added flavor, texture and color.

Broccoli Rice

Toss hot cooked rice with steamed broccoli. Season with sesame oil. Garnish with chopped cashews or toasted peanuts.

Little Bit of Italy

Combine prepared pesto sauce or marinara sauce with hot cooked rice. Top with Parmesan cheese.

Slightly Mexican

Top hot cooked rice with diced tomatoes, green onions, Monterey Jack cheese and cilantro.

It's Greek to Me

Toss toasted pecans and crumbled feta cheese with cooked rice.

Citrus Rice

Add grated orange, lemon or lime zest to hot cooked rice for a fresh, lively taste.

Rice Parmigiana

Add mixed vegetables, your favorite spice or herb, butter and Parmesan cheese to hot cooked rice.

Raspberry Rice Pudding

To cooled cooked rice, add fresh raspberries, honey and vanilla yogurt. Top with grated lemon zest.

Cinnamon Rice

Sprinkle cinnamon and brown sugar over hot cooked rice.

SOUPS AND SALADS

Sesame Rice Salad

- 1 can (15 ounces) mandarin orange segments, undrained
- 1 teaspoon ground ginger
- 2 cups Minute® Brown Rice, uncooked
- ½ cup Asian sesame salad dressing
- 3 green onions, thinly sliced
- 1 can (8 ounces) sliced water chestnuts, drained and chopped
- ½ cup sliced celery

Drain oranges, reserving liquid. Add enough water to reserved liquid to measure 1¾ cups. Stir in ginger. Prepare rice according to package directions, substituting 1¾ cups orange liquid for water. Refrigerate cooked rice 30 minutes. Add dressing, onions, water chestnuts and celery; mix lightly. Gently stir in oranges.

Serves 4

Pesto Rice Salad

2 cups Minute® White Rice, uncooked

1 package (7 ounces) basil pesto sauce

1 cup cherry tomatoes, halved

8 ounces whole-milk mozzarella cheese, cut into ½-inch cubes

⅓ cup shredded Parmesan cheese

Toasted pine nuts (optional)

Prepare rice according to package directions. Place in large bowl. Let stand 10 minutes. Add pesto sauce; mix well. Gently stir in tomatoes and cheese. Serve warm, or cover and refrigerate until ready to serve. Sprinkle with pine nuts, if desired.

Serves 6

Tips:

To toast pine nuts, spread in single layer in heavy-bottomed skillet. Cook over medium heat 1 to 2 minutes, stirring frequently, until nuts are lightly browned. Remove from skillet immediately. Cool before using.

For a heartier meal, add 1 package (6 ounces) grilled chicken breast strips to the prepared salad.

Spring Vegetable Rice Salad

2 cups Minute® White Rice, uncooked

1 cup halved cherry tomatoes

1 cup cut-up asparagus spears (1 inch long), cooked, cooled

1 cup light salad dressing

1 tablespoon Dijon mustard

1 tablespoon chopped fresh parsley

1 tablespoon grated lemon peel

1 tablespoon lemon juice

Prepare rice according to package directions. Toss rice with tomatoes and asparagus in medium bowl. Mix remaining ingredients until well blended. Add to rice mixture; toss to coat. Serve immediately, or cover and refrigerate until ready to serve.

Serves 8

Tip:

Asparagus spears snap off naturally where they are tough. To trim fresh asparagus, simply bend the spear near the bottom end, and it will break off at the right point.

Classic Rice Salad

2 cups Minute® White Rice, uncooked
½ cup chopped onion
½ cup sweet pickle relish
½ teaspoon salt
½ cup light mayonnaise
2 teaspoons mustard
¼ cup chopped pimentos
2 hard-cooked eggs, chopped
Lettuce leaves (optional)

Prepare rice according to package directions. Mix all ingredients. Chill. Serve on lettuce leaves, if desired.

Serves 6

Tip:

For perfect hard-cooked eggs, place the eggs in a single layer in a saucepan. Add enough cold water to cover the eggs by at least 1 inch. Cover and bring to a boil over high heat. Remove from the heat. Let eggs stand, covered, in the hot water 15 to17 minutes. Immediately pour off the water; cover the eggs with cold water or ice water and let stand until completely cooled before peeling.

Southwestern Rice Salad

2 cups Minute® White or Brown Rice, uncooked
1 can (15 ounces) black beans, drained, rinsed
1 cup corn
1 medium red bell pepper, chopped
3 green onions, sliced
1 cup Italian dressing
1 cup salsa
1 cup lightly crushed tortilla chips
Chopped fresh cilantro or parsley (optional)

Prepare rice according to package directions. Place
in large bowl; cool. Add beans, corn, bell pepper,
onions, dressing and salsa; mix lightly. Cover and
refrigerate at least 1 hour or until ready to serve. Top
with crushed chips and garnish with cilantro, if desired,
just before serving.

Serves 8

Waldorf Brown Rice Salad

1 cup Minute® Brown Rice, uncooked
3 medium apples
2 tablespoons lemon juice
½ cup chopped celery
½ cup chopped walnuts
½ cup raisins
½ cup fat-free mayonnaise
¾ cup nonfat vanilla yogurt
  Spring salad greens (optional)

Prepare rice according to package directions. Cool. Wash, core and dice apples, without peeling. Place apples in large bowl and toss with lemon juice. Add rice, celery, nuts and raisins; toss to combine. In medium bowl, combine mayonnaise and yogurt. Blend well. Fold into rice mixture. Serve over salad greens, if desired.

Serves 4

Confetti Beans and Rice with Chicken

1 cup Minute® Brown Rice, uncooked
2 teaspoons Dijon mustard
½ cup light Caesar salad dressing
1 can (15 ounces) black beans, drained, rinsed
12 ounces cooked chicken, diced
1 can (11 ounces) Mexican-style corn, drained
4 green onions, thinly sliced
4 large tomato halves, hollowed out
   Spinach leaves (optional)

Prepare rice according to package directions. Combine Dijon mustard and Caesar salad dressing in large bowl. Toss in rice, beans, chicken, corn and green onions. Fill tomatoes with rice mixture. Chill or serve at room temperature. Garnish with spinach leaves, if desired.

Serves 4

Chunky Chicken Vegetable Soup

1 teaspoon vegetable oil
½ pound boneless skinless chicken breasts, cut into ½-inch cubes
1 can (14½ ounces) chicken broth
2 cups water
2 cups assorted cut-up vegetables (sliced carrots, broccoli florets, chopped red pepper)*
1 packet Italian salad dressing and recipe mix
1 cup Minute® White Rice, uncooked
2 tablespoons chopped fresh parsley

Or substitute 1 package (10 ounces) frozen mixed vegetables, thawed.

Heat oil in large saucepan over medium-high heat. Add chicken; cook and stir until browned. Add broth, water, vegetables and salad dressing mix. Bring to a boil. Reduce heat to low; cover. Simmer 5 minutes. Stir in rice and parsley; cover. Remove from heat. Let stand 5 minutes.

Serves 4

Chicken Tortilla and Rice Soup

  2 cups Minute® White Rice, uncooked
  5 cups low-sodium chicken broth
  1 cup carrots, peeled and sliced thin
  1 can (10½ ounces) diced tomatoes with green
    chilies
  1 cup (6 ounces) cooked chicken breast, cubed
  1 tablespoon lime juice (optional)
 20 baked tortilla chips (about 1 cup), slightly
    crushed
  ½ cup shredded low-fat Mexican cheese blend
  ¼ cup chopped fresh cilantro
  1 avocado, diced (optional)

Prepare rice according to package directions. Bring broth to a boil in medium pot. Reduce heat and add carrots, tomatoes with chilies and chicken; simmer 10 minutes. Stir in rice; add lime juice, if desired. Divide equally into 6 serving bowls and top with tortilla chips, cheese, cilantro and avocado, if desired.

Serves 6

Tip:

To dice an avocado, insert a utility knife into the stem end. Slice in half lengthwise to the pit, turning the avocado while slicing. Remove the knife blade and twist the halves in opposite directions to pull apart. Press the knife blade into the pit, twisting the knife gently to pull the pit away from the avocado. Discard the pit. Cut the avocado flesh in a crisscross fashion to dice it, and then run a spoon underneath to scoop out the avocado pieces.

Louisiana Gumbo

2 cups Minute® White Rice, uncooked
2 tablespoons butter
2 tablespoons all-purpose flour
½ cup chopped onion
½ cup chopped celery
½ cup chopped green bell pepper
1 clove garlic, minced
1 package (14 ounces) smoked turkey sausage, sliced
1 can (14½ ounces) diced tomatoes
1 can (13¾ ounces) condensed chicken broth
1 package (10 ounces) frozen sliced okra, thawed*
1 tablespoon Cajun seasoning
¼ teaspoon dried thyme
½ pound shrimp, peeled, deveined
Salt and black pepper, to taste

Or substitute 1 package (10 ounces) frozen cut green beans.

Prepare rice according to package directions. Melt butter in large skillet over medium-high heat. Stir in flour; cook and stir until light golden brown, about 5 minutes. Add onions, celery, bell pepper and garlic; cook 2 to 3 minutes or until tender. Stir in sausage, tomatoes, broth, okra, seasoning and thyme; cover. Simmer 5 minutes, stirring occasionally. Add shrimp; cook 5 minutes or until shrimp are pink. Season with salt and pepper to taste. Serve with rice.

Serves 6

Spicy Beef and Bean Chili

- 2 cups Minute® White Rice, uncooked
- 1 tablespoon vegetable oil
- 1 pound boneless beef chuck steak, cut into bite-sized pieces
- 2 cups chopped onion
- ⅓ cup spicy steak sauce
- 1 can (14½ ounces) diced tomatoes, undrained
- 1 can (15¼ ounces) red kidney beans, drained, rinsed*

*Or substitute canned pinto beans.

Prepare rice according to package directions. Heat oil in Dutch oven or large saucepan over medium-high heat. Add beef and onions; cook and stir 4 to 5 minutes or until meat is evenly browned. Add steak sauce and tomatoes; mix well. Bring to a boil. Reduce heat to medium-low; simmer 30 to 40 minutes or until meat is tender. Stir in beans. Cook until heated through, stirring occasionally. Serve over rice.

Serves 4

Tip:

Spoon meat mixture and rice onto warmed flour tortillas, and then top with sour cream and roll up.

Broccoli, Cheese and Rice Soup

2 cups Minute® White or Brown Rice, uncooked
1 package (10 ounces) frozen chopped
   broccoli, thawed
1 can (10¾ ounces) reduced-fat cream of
   mushroom soup
3 cups low-fat milk
1 pound low-fat processed cheese, cubed
   Shredded cheese (optional)

Prepare rice according to package directions. Combine broccoli, soup and milk in medium saucepan. Bring to simmer over medium heat. Add cheese and stir until melted. Remove from heat and stir in rice. Top with additional cheese, if desired.

Serves 6

Easy Santa Fe Style Stuffed Peppers

1 cup Minute® Brown Rice, uncooked
  Nonstick cooking spray
1 pound lean ground beef*
1 package (10 ounces) frozen whole-kernel corn
1½ cups chunky salsa
4 large bell peppers, tops and seeds removed
1 cup shredded Colby and Monterey Jack
  cheese

Or substitute ground turkey.

Prepare rice according to package directions. Preheat oven to 425°F. Spray large nonstick skillet with nonstick cooking spray. Add meat and brown over medium heat; drain excess fat. Stir in corn, salsa and rice. Pierce peppers with fork or sharp knife; place in baking dish. Fill peppers with meat mixture. Cover with foil. Bake 20 minutes. Uncover. Sprinkle with cheese before serving.

Serves 4

Krab and Rice Primavera

2 cups frozen broccoli, cauliflower and carrot blend*

¼ cup water

2½ cups fat-free milk

1 package (8 ounces) imitation crabmeat

1 tablespoon butter or margarine

¼ teaspoon garlic powder

1½ cups Minute® White Rice, uncooked

½ cup grated Parmesan cheese

*Or substitute your favorite frozen vegetable blend.

Bring vegetables and water to a boil in medium saucepan, stirring occasionally. Reduce heat; cover. Simmer 3 minutes. Add milk, imitation crabmeat, butter and garlic powder. Bring to a full boil. Stir in rice and Parmesan cheese; cover. Remove from heat. Let stand 5 minutes. Fluff with fork.

Serves 6

Tip:

Substitute fresh cooked crabmeat, shrimp or scallops.

Italian Beef Wraps

½ **pound thin lean beef strips***
¼ **teaspoon black pepper**
   Nonstick cooking spray
1 **large yellow onion, halved, sliced**
1 **medium green bell pepper, thinly sliced**
1 **medium red bell pepper, thinly sliced**
1 **packet Italian salad dressing and recipe mix**
1¼ **cups water**
1 **cup Minute® Brown Rice, uncooked**
4 **(8-inch) flour tortillas, warmed**
   Light sour cream (optional)

*Purchase beef strips already cut for stir-fry.

Season meat with pepper. Spray large nonstick skillet with nonstick cooking spray. Add meat; cook 5 minutes or until cooked through. Remove meat from skillet; cover to keep warm. Add onions, bell peppers, salad dressing mix and water to skillet. Bring to a boil. Stir in rice; cover. Reduce heat to medium-low; simmer 5 minutes. Remove from heat. Add meat mixture; stir. Let stand, covered, 5 minutes. Spoon meat mixture evenly onto tortillas and top with sour cream, if desired; roll up.

Serves 4

Rosemary Pork Chops

1 tablespoon vegetable oil

4 pork chops

1 small onion, chopped

2 cups Minute® White Rice, uncooked

1 cup roasted red peppers, drained, chopped

1 can (14½ ounces) beef broth

¼ cup balsamic vinaigrette dressing

½ teaspoon dried rosemary

Heat oil in large nonstick skillet over medium-high heat. Add chops; cook 6 minutes, turning after 3 minutes. Remove from skillet; cover to keep warm. Add onions to skillet. Cook 5 minutes or until onions are tender, stirring occasionally. Stir in rice, peppers, broth, dressing and rosemary. Bring to a boil. Reduce heat to medium-low; simmer 5 minutes. Serve chops with rice.

Serves 4

Tip:

Serve with hot steamed broccoli.

Tex-Mex Bake

1   cup Minute® White or Brown Rice, uncooked
1   pound ground beef
1   can (15 ounces) chili beans
1   can (10 ounces) diced tomatoes with green
      chilies
1   bag (12 ounces) crushed tortilla chips
1   pound prepared cheese product, cut into
      cubes, divided
     Sliced green onions and sour cream (optional)

Preheat oven to 350°F. Prepare rice according to
package directions; set aside. Brown meat in large
nonstick skillet over medium heat; drain off excess fat.
Mix in cooked rice, beans and tomatoes with chilies.
Cover bottom of baking dish with chips. Layer half
of cheese over chips. Top with rice mixture. Top with
remaining cheese. Bake, uncovered, 15 minutes or
until cheese is melted. Garnish with green onions and
sour cream, if desired.

Serves 8

Green Bean, Chicken and Rice Dinner

1 tablespoon vegetable oil
4 small boneless skinless chicken breasts*
2 cups frozen cut green beans, thawed
1¾ cups milk
1 can (10¾ ounces) condensed cream of mushroom soup
¼ teaspoon paprika
¼ teaspoon black pepper
2 cups Minute® White Rice, uncooked
½ cup canned French-fried onion rings

*Or substitute 12 ounces cooked diced chicken.

Heat oil in large nonstick skillet over medium-high heat. Add chicken; cover. Cook 4 minutes on each side or until cooked through (170°F). Remove chicken from skillet; cover to keep warm. Add beans, milk, soup, and seasonings to skillet; stir. Bring to a boil. Stir in rice. Top with chicken; cover. Reduce heat to low; cook 5 minutes or until rice is tender. Sprinkle with onion rings.

Serves 4

Chili and Rice Dinner

Nonstick cooking spray

1 pound lean ground beef*

1 can (15½ ounces) kidney beans, drained

1 can (14½ ounces) diced tomatoes, undrained

1 can (8 ounces) tomato sauce

2 cups water

1 packet (1¼ ounces) chili seasoning mix**

2 cups Minute® White Rice, uncooked

*Or substitute ground turkey.

**Or substitute 1 teaspoon chili powder, ½ teaspoon garlic powder, ½ teaspoon ground cumin and ¼ teaspoon salt.

Spray large nonstick skillet with nonstick cooking spray. Add meat and brown over medium heat; drain off excess fat. Add beans, tomatoes, tomato sauce, water and seasoning mix; stir. Bring to a boil. Stir in rice; cover. Reduce heat to low; cook 5 minutes. Stir before serving.

Serves 6

Tip:

Prepare with chicken or omit meat for a meatless dish.

Piña Colada Shrimp and Rice

1 **tablespoon olive oil**
1 **pound large shrimp, peeled, deveined**
1 **cup pineapple juice**
1 **can (20 ounces) pineapple chunks, drained**
1 **can (13½ ounces) light coconut milk***
3 **cups Minute® White Rice, uncooked**
¼ **cup shredded coconut**
1 **green onion, sliced**

**Do not substitute cream of coconut;
light coconut milk can be found in the
supermarket's ethnic foods section.*

Heat oil in large skillet over
medium-high heat. Add shrimp;
cook and stir 4 minutes until almost
cooked through. Add pineapple
juice, pineapple chunks and
coconut milk; bring to boil. Stir in
rice; cover. Remove from heat. Let
stand 5 minutes. (If all liquid has not been absorbed,
cook on low heat an additional 2 minutes or until liquid
is absorbed.) Fluff with fork. Spoon into serving dishes;
sprinkle with coconut and green onions.

Serves 6

Tip:

*For extra flavor, toast the shredded coconut. Preheat the
oven to 350°F. Spread coconut evenly in shallow baking
pan. Bake 8 to 10 minutes or until lightly toasted, stirring
occasionally. Watch carefully as coconut can easily burn.*

Chicken and Rice Florentine

1 tablespoon vegetable oil

4 small boneless skinless chicken breasts

2 cups water

1 can (10¾ ounces) condensed cream of
   chicken soup

⅛ teaspoon ground nutmeg (optional)

2 cups Minute® Brown Rice, uncooked

1 package (10 ounces) frozen chopped
   spinach, thawed, well drained*

1 cup shredded Parmesan cheese**

*Or substitute 1½ cups chopped fresh spinach or 1 can (13½
ounces) chopped spinach, well drained.*

**Or substitute 1 cup shredded Swiss cheese or shredded Cheddar
cheese.*

Heat oil in large nonstick skillet over medium-high heat.
Add chicken; cover. Cook 4 minutes on each side or
until cooked through (170°F). Remove chicken from
skillet; cover to keep warm. Add water, soup and
nutmeg, if desired, to skillet; stir. Bring to a boil. Stir
in rice, spinach and cheese. Top with chicken; cover.
Reduce heat to low; cook 5 minutes. Let stand 5
minutes.

Serves 4

Aloha Pork Chop Skillet

1   tablespoon vegetable oil
4   pork chops
1   medium red bell pepper, cut into chunks
1   medium yellow bell pepper, cut into chunks
2   cans (8 ounces each) pineapple chunks in
     juice, undrained
½   cup fat-free reduced-sodium chicken broth
¼   cup sweet-and-sour sauce
1½ teaspoons garlic powder
2   cups Minute® White Rice, uncooked

Heat oil in large nonstick skillet over medium-high heat. Add chops; cook 5 minutes on each side or until browned. Remove chops; cover to keep warm. Add bell peppers, pineapple, broth, sauce and garlic powder to skillet; mix well. Bring to a boil. Stir in rice. Top with chops; cover. Reduce heat to medium-low; simmer 5 minutes or until chops are cooked through (160°F). Remove from heat; let stand 5 minutes.

Serves 4

Tip:

*Substitute 4 small boneless skinless chicken breasts.
Prepare as directed, increasing browning time to 6 minutes
on each side or until cooked through (170°F).*

Cheesy Chicken and Asparagus Rice Dinner

1 tablespoon vegetable oil

4 small boneless skinless chicken breasts

⅛ teaspoon black pepper

1½ cups water or milk

1 can (10¾ ounces) condensed cream of chicken soup

2 cups Minute® White Rice, uncooked

2 cups cut-up fresh asparagus*

1 cup shredded Cheddar cheese

¼ cup sliced almonds

Or substitute 1 package (10 ounces) thawed frozen asparagus cuts.

Heat oil in large nonstick skillet over medium-high heat. Add chicken; season with pepper. Cover; cook 4 minutes on each side or until chicken is cooked through (170°F). Remove chicken from skillet; cover to keep warm. Add water and soup to skillet; stir until well blended. Bring to a boil. Stir in rice and asparagus; top with chicken. Sprinkle with cheese and almonds; cover. Reduce heat to low; cook 5 minutes.

Serves 4

Tip:

For extra flavor, toast the almonds. Preheat oven to 350°F. Spread almonds evenly in a shallow baking pan. Bake 5 minutes or until lightly browned. Stir once during baking.

One-Pan Taco Dinner

Nonstick cooking spray
1 **pound lean ground beef**
1 **packet (1¼ ounces) taco seasoning mix**
2 **cups water**
2 **cups Minute® White Rice, uncooked**
1 **cup shredded Cheddar cheese**
2 **cups shredded lettuce**
1 **large tomato, chopped**
Salsa (optional)

Spray large nonstick skillet with nonstick cooking spray. Add meat and brown over medium-high heat; drain off excess fat. Add seasoning mix and water; stir. Bring to a boil. Stir in rice. Sprinkle with cheese; cover. Reduce heat to low; simmer 5 minutes. Top with lettuce and tomato just before serving. Serve with salsa, if desired.

Serves 4

Tip:
No need to use serving utensils. Serve with tortilla chips instead of forks!

Hoppin' John

1 package (14 ounces) smoked turkey sausage, thinly sliced

3 cans (15½ ounces each) black-eyed peas, drained, rinsed

2 cans (14½ ounces each) chicken broth

2 cups chopped onion

1 teaspoon crushed red pepper

½ teaspoon ground red pepper

2½ cups Minute® White Rice, uncooked

Chopped fresh parsley (optional)

Brown sausage in medium saucepan over medium-high heat. Add peas, broth, onions and seasonings; bring to a boil. Stir in rice; cover. Simmer 10 minutes or until rice is tender. Garnish with parsley, if desired.

Serves 8

Pepper Steak

2 cups Minute® White Rice, uncooked

1 boneless beef sirloin steak (1 pound), ½ inch thick, fat trimmed*

½ teaspoon garlic powder

¼ teaspoon black pepper

1 tablespoon vegetable oil

1 medium green bell pepper, cut into strips

1 medium red bell pepper, cut into strips

1 medium onion, sliced (optional)

1 cup light teriyaki sauce

1 tablespoon cornstarch

Or substitute 1 pound boneless skinless chicken breasts.

Prepare rice according to package directions. Slice steak into thin strips; season with garlic powder and pepper. Heat oil in large nonstick skillet over medium-high heat. Add beef; cook and stir 4 to 5 minutes or until cooked through. Add bell peppers and onions, if desired, and cook until crisp-tender. Combine teriyaki sauce and cornstarch, and add to beef mixture. Bring to a boil, stirring constantly. Simmer 2 minutes, or until sauce thickens slightly. Serve over rice.

Serves 4

Amazin' Crab Rice Cakes

1 cup chicken broth
1 cup Minute® White Rice, uncooked
2 eggs
2 cans (6 ounces each) crabmeat, drained, flaked*
2 tablespoons seafood seasoning
¼ cup (½ stick) butter or margarine
Fresh lemon wedges (optional)

*Or substitute 12 ounces canned salmon.

Bring broth to a boil in small saucepan. Stir in rice; cover. Remove from heat; let stand 5 minutes. Fluff with fork. Beat eggs lightly in medium bowl. Add rice, crabmeat and seasoning; mix well. Refrigerate 5 minutes. Shape into 8 patties. Melt butter in large skillet over medium heat. Add patties; cook 5 minutes on each side or until golden brown and heated through. Serve with lemon, if desired.

Serves 4

Tip:

To serve as appetizers, make patties bite-sized.

Savory Chicken Pot Pie

1   tablespoon olive oil
½ cup chopped onion
8   ounces sliced mushrooms
2   cups frozen mixed vegetables*
6   ounces cooked chicken, diced
2   cans (10½ ounces each) condensed cream of
      chicken soup
2   cans (14½ ounces each) chicken broth
3   cups Minute® White Rice, uncooked
1   can (8 count) large flaky biscuits

Or substitute 1 can (15 ounces) mixed vegetables, drained.

Heat oil in large saucepan over medium-high heat. Add onions and mushrooms; cook and stir 5 minutes. Mix in remaining ingredients, except rice and biscuits; bring to a boil. Stir in rice. Pour into 13×9-inch baking dish. Separate biscuits and place on top of filling. Bake 10 to 12 minutes, or until biscuits are golden brown.

Serves 8

Tip:
Use cooked turkey and turkey broth to make turkey pot pie.

Fiesta Shrimp Creole

2 cups Minute® White or Brown Rice, uncooked
2 tablespoons vegetable oil
2 tablespoons all-purpose flour
1 small green bell pepper, chopped
2 stalks celery, chopped
2 cloves garlic, minced
1 jar (16 ounces) chunky salsa
1 can (8 ounces) tomato sauce
1 teaspoon hot pepper sauce (optional)
1½ pounds shrimp, peeled, deveined*

Or substitute fresh boneless skinless chicken, cut into ½-inch pieces.

Prepare rice according to package directions. Mix oil and flour in large saucepan. Cook over medium heat 6 to 8 minutes or until browned, stirring constantly. Add bell pepper, celery and garlic; cook and stir 4 minutes or until tender. Stir in salsa, tomato sauce and pepper sauce, if desired; simmer 10 minutes, stirring occasionally. Stir in shrimp; cook 6 to 8 minutes or until shrimp are cooked through. Serve over rice.

Serves 6

Jambalaya Skillet

1 medium green bell pepper, chopped
½ cup chopped onion
½ cup chopped celery
1 tablespoon vegetable oil
1 pound boneless skinless chicken breasts, cut into strips
2 tablespoons Creole seasoning, divided
1 can (14½ ounces) diced tomatoes, undrained
1 cup water
1 can (8 ounces) tomato sauce
½ pound medium shrimp, peeled, deveined
2 cups Minute® Brown Rice, uncooked

Heat oil in large nonstick skillet over medium-high heat. Add bell pepper, onions and celery; cook and stir until crisp-tender. Toss chicken with 1 tablespoon seasoning. Add to skillet. Cook and stir 2 to 3 minutes or until cooked through. Add tomatoes, water, tomato sauce, shrimp and remaining 1 tablespoon seasoning; mix well. Bring to a boil. Stir in rice; cover. Simmer 5 minutes. Remove from heat. Let stand 5 minutes. Fluff with fork.

Serves 6

Tip:

Omit 1 tablespoon Creole seasoning. Substitute 2 packages (6 ounces each) grilled chicken breast strips for fresh chicken strips. Cook and stir bell pepper, onions, celery and chicken breast strips in hot oil until vegetables are crisp-tender. Continue as directed.

Chicken à la King

- 1 cup Minute® White Rice, uncooked
- ⅓ cup salad dressing
- 2 tablespoons all-purpose flour
- 1 cup milk
- 2 packages (6 ounces each) roasted chicken breast strips, diced
- 1 cup sliced mushrooms*
- 1 cup frozen peas*
- ½ medium red bell pepper, chopped*
- Dash black pepper

*Or substitute your favorite frozen vegetable blend.

Prepare rice according to package directions. Mix salad dressing, flour and milk in medium saucepan. Bring to a boil, stirring constantly. Reduce heat and cook until thickened, about 1 minute. Stir in all remaining ingredients except rice; cook 10 minutes or until vegetables are tender. Serve over rice.

Serves 4

Tip:

For a healthier alternative, prepare with light mayonnaise and fat-free milk.

Classic Beef Stroganoff

1 cup Minute® White Rice, uncooked
1 tablespoon vegetable oil
1 cup chopped onion
1 pound lean ground beef
2 cups sliced mushrooms
1 can (14½ ounces) beef broth
1 tablespoon Worcestershire sauce
1 can (10¾ ounces) cream of mushroom soup
½ cup sour cream

Prepare rice according to package directions. Heat oil in medium skillet over medium-high heat. Add onions and cook and stir 3 minutes. Add beef and brown; drain off excess fat. Add mushrooms, broth, Worcestershire sauce and soup. Bring to a boil and simmer 5 minutes. Stir in sour cream. Serve over rice.

Serves 4

Cashew Chicken Dijon

2 cups Minute® White Rice, uncooked

2 tablespoons vegetable oil, divided

1 medium green bell pepper, cut into strips

1 medium red bell pepper, cut into strips

1 pound boneless skinless chicken breasts, cut into thin strips

1 cup low-sodium chicken broth

¼ cup Dijon mustard

1 teaspoon cornstarch

¼ cup cashews, coarsely chopped

Prepare rice according to package directions. Heat 1 tablespoon oil in large skillet over high heat. Add bell peppers; cook and stir until crisp-tender. Remove from skillet; cover to keep warm. Add remaining 1 tablespoon oil and chicken to skillet; cook and stir until chicken is cooked through. Remove from skillet; cover to keep warm. Mix broth, mustard and cornstarch. Add to skillet; cook on medium-high heat until thickened, stirring constantly. Return chicken and peppers to skillet; cook and stir 2 minutes or until heated through. Stir in cashews. Serve over rice.

Serves 6

Tip:
Cut chicken into strips while still slightly frozen.

Beef and Broccoli Stir-Fry

2 cups Minute® Brown Rice, uncooked

1 pound beef flank steak, cut into strips

2 teaspoons cornstarch

¼ cup orange juice

1 teaspoon ground ginger

1 tablespoon vegetable oil

1 package (10 ounces) frozen broccoli florets, thawed

1 can (8 ounces) sliced water chestnuts, drained

¼ cup reduced-sodium soy sauce

¼ cup dry-roasted peanuts (optional)

Prepare rice according to package directions. Place steak strips in medium bowl. Sprinkle with cornstarch; toss to coat. Add orange juice and ginger; stir until well blended. Heat oil in large nonstick skillet over medium-high heat. Add steak mixture; stir-fry 4 to 5 minutes or until steak is cooked through. Reduce heat to medium-low. Add broccoli, water chestnuts and soy sauce; mix well. Cover; simmer 5 minutes or until thickened, stirring frequently. Serve over rice; sprinkle with peanuts, if desired.

Serves 4

Tip:

To make slicing easier, place steak in freezer for 30 minutes to 1 hour before cutting into strips.

Greek-Style Lemon Chicken

1 tablespoon olive oil

1 pound boneless skinless chicken breasts, cut into strips

2 cloves garlic, minced

2 cups Minute® Brown or White Rice, uncooked

1 can (14½ ounces) chicken broth

½ cup matchstick or grated carrots

¼ cup sliced pitted ripe olives

1 tablespoon grated lemon peel

1 tablespoon parsley flakes

Crumbled feta cheese (optional)

Lemon wedges (optional)

Heat oil in large nonstick skillet over medium-high heat. Add chicken; cook and stir 6 to 8 minutes or until chicken is cooked through, adding garlic during last 3 minutes of cooking time. Add remaining ingredients except cheese and lemon wedges; stir until well blended. Bring to a boil; cover. Remove from heat. Let stand 5 minutes. Sprinkle on feta cheese and serve with lemon wedges, if desired.

Serves 4

Teriyaki Steak and Brown Rice Dinner

1 **tablespoon vegetable oil**
1 **pound boneless beef sirloin steak, cut into strips***
1 **teaspoon garlic powder**
2 **cups water**
⅓ **cup teriyaki sauce****
2 **cups Minute® Brown Rice, uncooked**
4 **cups broccoli florets**
1 **large red bell pepper, cut into strips**

Or substitute 1 pound boneless skinless chicken breasts, cut into strips.

**Or substitute ¼ cup soy sauce plus 2 tablespoons water.*

Heat oil in large nonstick skillet over medium-high heat. Sprinkle steak with garlic powder; add to skillet and cook and stir 5 minutes or until steak is cooked through. Stir in water and teriyaki sauce; bring to a boil. Stir in rice, broccoli and bell pepper. Return to a boil. Reduce heat to low; cover. Simmer 5 minutes. Remove from heat. Let stand 5 minutes. Fluff with fork.

Serves 4

Spanish Chicken and Rice

1 tablespoon olive oil

1 pound boneless skinless chicken breasts, diced

1 medium onion, chopped

1 medium red bell pepper, chopped

1 cup chicken broth

1 can (15 ounces) Spanish-style diced
   tomatoes, undrained

1 cup frozen peas

1 teaspoon garlic powder

1 teaspoon turmeric (optional)

2 cups Minute® White Rice, uncooked

Heat oil in large skillet over medium-high heat. Cook chicken, onions and bell peppers until chicken is browned, stirring occasionally. Add broth, tomatoes, peas, garlic powder and turmeric, if desired; bring to a boil. Stir in rice. Reduce heat to low; cover. Cook 5 minutes or until rice is tender.

Serves 4

Tip:

*To make Easy Paella with Shrimp, add
½ pound peeled and deveined medium
shrimp at the same time as the broth.*

Cheesy Mexican Chicken

2 cups diced cooked chicken

1 can (10¾ ounces) low-sodium cream of chicken soup

1½ cups shredded mild Cheddar cheese, divided*

1 cup milk

1 packet (1¼ ounces) taco seasoning mix

1 cup Minute® White Rice, uncooked

2 cups tortilla chips, crushed

Or use your favorite Mexican-style shredded cheese.

Preheat oven to 375°F. Mix chicken, soup, 1 cup cheese, milk and seasoning mix in medium saucepan. Bring to a boil. Remove from heat and stir in rice. Pour into 2-quart baking dish. Top with chips. Bake 15 minutes. Remove from oven and sprinkle with remaining ½ cup cheese.

Serves 4

Tip:

When a recipe calls for chopped cooked chicken, it can be difficult to judge how much chicken to purchase. As a guideline, 2 whole chicken breasts (about 10 ounces each) will yield about 2 cups of chopped cooked chicken.

Rice Lasagna

Nonstick cooking spray
1 cup Minute® White Rice, uncooked
2 eggs, slightly beaten
¾ cup grated Parmesan cheese, divided
2 cups shredded Mozzarella cheese
½ cup cottage cheese
1 pound lean ground beef
1 jar (15½ ounces) spaghetti sauce
½ teaspoon garlic powder

Preheat oven to 375°F. Coat 13×9-inch baking dish with nonstick cooking spray; set aside. Prepare rice according to package directions. Cool slightly. Combine rice, eggs and ¼ cup Parmesan cheese in medium bowl. Mix well; set aside. Combine ¼ cup Parmesan cheese, mozzarella cheese and cottage cheese in separate bowl. Mix well; set aside. Spray large nonstick skillet with nonstick cooking spray. Add meat and brown over medium heat; drain off excess fat. Add spaghetti sauce and garlic powder; continue cooking until thoroughly heated. Spoon one-half of rice mixture into baking dish. Cover with one-half of cheese mixture. Top with one-half of meat sauce. Repeat layers. Top with remaining ¼ cup Parmesan cheese. Bake 15 to 20 minutes or until thoroughly heated.

Serves 6 to 8

Chicken Carbonara Risotto

1 tablespoon vegetable oil

1 pound boneless skinless chicken breasts, cut into strips

1 can (10¾ ounces) condensed cream of chicken soup

1 cup frozen peas

1½ cups milk

2 cups Minute® White Rice, uncooked

¼ cup real bacon bits

¼ cup grated Parmesan cheese*

*Or substitute grated Romano cheese.

Heat oil in large skillet over medium-high heat. Add chicken; cook and stir 4 to 5 minutes or until cooked through. Add soup, peas and milk; bring to a boil. Stir in rice; cover. Reduce heat to medium-low; simmer 5 minutes. Stir in bacon bits and Parmesan cheese.

Serves 4

Chicken with Basil Cream Sauce

1 cup Minute® Brown Rice, uncooked
½ cup fat-free mayonnaise
½ cup fat-free milk
1 teaspoon dried basil or 2 tablespoons fresh basil, chopped
2 packages (6 ounces each) roasted chicken breast strips
1 medium tomato, chopped
1 green onion, sliced

Prepare rice according to package directions. Mix mayonnaise, milk and basil in medium saucepan; cook 2 minutes or until heated through and slightly thickened, stirring occasionally. Stir in chicken and cook until heated through. Spoon rice onto serving platter; top with chicken and sauce. Sprinkle with tomato and onions.

Serves 4

Tip:

Chopped fresh basil tends to bruise and discolor easily. To avoid this, stack the leaves together and roll them up cigar-style. Use a sharp knife to cut the leaves crosswise into strips, then make several cross cuts to finish chopping.

Fried Rice

- 1 tablespoon vegetable oil
- 3 eggs, lightly beaten
- 1 can (14½ ounces) chicken broth
- 1 package (16 ounces) frozen stir-fry vegetables, thawed
- 2 tablespoons soy sauce
- 2 cups Minute® White Rice, uncooked

Heat oil in large skillet over medium heat. Add eggs; scramble until done. Remove from skillet; cover to keep warm. Add broth, vegetables and soy sauce to skillet; bring to a boil. Stir in rice; cover. Remove from heat. Let stand 5 minutes. Stir in scrambled eggs. Serve immediately.

Serves 4

Rice and Cranberry Pilaf

1 cup chicken broth

1 cup white cranberry juice

2 cups Minute® White Rice, uncooked

¼ cup dried cranberries

¼ cup sliced almonds, toasted

1 teaspoon orange peel (optional)

Pour broth and juice into medium saucepan. Bring to a boil over medium-high heat. Stir in rice and cranberries; return to a boil. Cover; remove from heat. Let stand 5 minutes. Stir in almonds. Top with orange peel, if desired.

Serves 6

Tip:

To toast almonds quickly, spread them in a single layer in heavy-bottomed skillet. Cook over medium heat 1 to 2 minutes, stirring frequently, until nuts are lightly browned. Remove from skillet immediately. Cool before using.

Quick Brown Rice and Mushroom Pilaf

2 tablespoons olive oil
1 small onion, chopped
¼ cup chopped celery
1½ cups sliced mushrooms
1 can (14½ ounces) chicken broth
2 cups Minute® Brown Rice, uncooked
½ cup chopped walnuts, toasted
2 tablespoons chopped fresh parsley

Heat oil in medium saucepan over medium heat. Add onions and celery; cook 3 minutes or until crisp-tender, stirring occasionally. Add mushrooms; cook 3 minutes or until mushrooms are tender, stirring occasionally. Add broth; stir. Bring to a boil. Stir in rice; cover. Reduce heat to medium-low; simmer 5 minutes. Remove from heat; let stand 5 minutes. Add walnuts and parsley; mix lightly.

Serves 8

Cheesy Rice and Broccoli

3 cups fresh broccoli florets*
2 cups chicken broth
2 cups Minute® White Rice, uncooked
½ pound (8 ounces) reduced-fat prepared
    cheese product, cut up

Or substitute frozen broccoli florets.

Place broccoli and broth in medium saucepan. Bring to a boil over medium-high heat. Stir in rice; cover. Remove from heat. Let stand 5 minutes. Stir in cheese; cover. Let stand 5 minutes. Stir until cheese is melted.

Serves 8

Red Beans and Rice

1 tablespoon butter or margarine

½ medium green bell pepper, chopped

½ medium onion, chopped

1 can (14½ ounces) beef broth

1 can (15½ ounces) red kidney beans, drained, rinsed

1 tablespoon Cajun seasoning

2 cups Minute® White Rice, uncooked

Hot pepper sauce (optional)

Melt butter in large skillet over medium heat. Add bell pepper and onions; cook and stir until crisp-tender. Add

broth, beans and seasoning; stir. Bring to a boil. Stir in rice; cover. Remove from heat. Let stand 5 minutes. Fluff with fork. Serve with pepper sauce, if desired.

Serves 4

Tip:

To turn this dish into a quick meal, add 2 cups diced ham or cooked sausage at the same time as the broth.

Cajun Dirty Rice

½ pound pork
  sausage,
  crumbled

1 small onion, finely
  chopped

1 stalk celery, finely
  chopped

1 small clove garlic,
  minced

2 cups chicken
  broth

1 tablespoon Cajun
  seasoning

2 cups Minute®
  White Rice,
  uncooked

Cook sausage in medium skillet over medium heat until evenly browned, stirring occasionally. Add onions, celery and garlic; cook and stir 5 minutes or until sausage is cooked through and vegetables are tender. Add broth to skillet with seasoning; stir. Bring to a boil. Stir in rice; cover. Remove from heat. Let stand 5 minutes. Fluff with fork.

Serves 6

Tip:

For a more authentic dish, reduce sausage to ¼ pound and add ¼ pound chopped chicken livers.

Cheesy Rice 'n Tomatoes

1 tablespoon vegetable oil
½ cup chopped onion
2 cups Minute® White Rice, uncooked
2 cups chicken broth
2 small tomatoes, chopped
1 package (8 ounces) cream cheese
¼ cup shredded Parmesan cheese
1 tablespoon chopped fresh parsley

Heat oil in medium saucepan over medium heat. Add onions; cook and stir 3 minutes or until tender. Stir in rice, broth and tomatoes. Bring to a boil. Reduce heat to low; simmer 3 minutes. Add cheeses and parsley; stir until blended. Remove from heat. Let stand, covered, 5 minutes before serving.

Serves 4

Tip:

For a main dish, add 1 pound cooked, peeled shrimp.

Creamy Lemon-Asparagus Risotto

2 tablespoons olive oil
1 medium onion, finely chopped
2 cups Minute® White Rice, uncooked
½ pound fresh asparagus, cut into 2-inch lengths
2 cups chicken broth
2 tablespoons light cream cheese
 Grated peel and juice from ½ medium lemon

Heat oil in large skillet over medium heat. Add onions; cook and stir 2 minutes or until tender. Stir in rice, asparagus and broth. Bring to a boil. Reduce heat to low; simmer 5 minutes. Add cream cheese, lemon peel and juice; stir until well blended.

Serves 6

Tip:
Substitute ½ cup dry white wine for an equal amount of broth.

Dijon Rice Florentine

1 can (14½ ounces) chicken broth
1 clove garlic, minced
1 cup Minute® White Rice, uncooked
1 package (10 ounces) frozen chopped
    spinach, thawed, well drained
2 tablespoons Dijon mustard
2 tablespoons grated Parmesan cheese

Bring broth and garlic to a boil in medium saucepan over high heat. Add rice; stir. Reduce heat to low; cover. Cook 10 minutes. Add spinach and mustard; stir. Cook, uncovered, an additional 8 to 10 minutes or until liquid is absorbed and rice is tender. Stir in cheese.

Serves 4

Cheesy Rice and Corn Casserole

2 cups Minute® White Rice, uncooked

2 cups chicken broth

8 ounces chive-and-onion cream cheese spread

1 can (15¼ ounces) corn with red and green bell peppers, drained

1 cup shredded Mexican-style four-cheese blend, divided

2 tablespoons chopped fresh cilantro

Preheat oven to 375°F. Prepare rice according to package directions, using broth for water. Mix rice, cream cheese spread, corn, ¾ cup shredded cheese and cilantro. Pour mixture into greased 1½-quart baking dish. Sprinkle with remaining ¼ cup shredded cheese. Bake 15 to 20 minutes or until cheese on top is melted and lightly browned.

Serves 6

Tip:

For more Mexican flavor, add 1 to 2 teaspoons ground cumin.

Cheesy Tuna Dinner

- 1 can (10¾ ounces) condensed cream of mushroom soup
- 1½ cups milk
- 2 cans (6 ounces each) tuna, drained, flaked
- 1 cup frozen green peas, thawed
- 2 cups Minute® White Rice, uncooked
- 1 cup shredded Cheddar cheese
  Canned French-fried onions or crushed potato chips (optional)

Mix soup and milk in medium saucepan. Bring to a boil over medium heat, stirring frequently. Add tuna and peas; mix well. Return to a boil. Stir in rice and cheese; cover. Reduce heat to low; cook 5 minutes. Stir until cheese is melted. Garnish with onions or chips, if desired.

Serves 4

Easy Chicken and Rice Tacos

    1 tablespoon butter or margarine
    1 pound ground chicken or turkey
    1 small onion, chopped
    1 packet (1 ¼ ounces) taco seasoning mix
 1 ¼ cups water
    1 can (8 ounces) tomato sauce
 1 ½ cups Minute® White Rice, uncooked
    1 can (15 ounces) kidney beans, drained, rinsed
   16 taco shells, heated
    1 package (8 ounces) shredded Cheddar cheese
    1 cup shredded lettuce
    2 medium tomatoes, chopped

Melt butter in large skillet over medium-high heat.
Add chicken and onions; cook and stir until chicken
is cooked through. Stir in seasoning mix, water and
tomato sauce. Bring to a boil. Reduce heat to low;
cover. Simmer 5 minutes. Add rice and beans; mix
well. Cover; remove from heat. Let stand 5 minutes.
Fill taco shells evenly with chicken mixture; top with
cheese, lettuce and tomatoes.

Serves 8

Porcupine Meatballs

1 tablespoon butter or margarine
1 small onion, chopped
1 pound lean ground beef*
1 cup Minute® White Rice, uncooked
1 egg, lightly beaten
1 small packet meatloaf seasoning
¼ cup water
1 jar (15½ ounces or larger) spaghetti sauce

Or substitute ground turkey.

Melt butter in small skillet over medium-high heat. Add onions; cook and stir until tender. Place onions, meat, rice, egg and seasoning in large bowl. Add water; mix until well blended. Shape into medium-sized meatballs. Pour spaghetti sauce into skillet. Bring to a boil. Add meatballs; return to a boil. Reduce heat to low; cover. Simmer 15 minutes or until meatballs are cooked through.

Serves 4

Tip:
Round out each serving with ½ cup hot cooked rice and a serving of your kids' favorite vegetables.

Skillet Pizza

2 cups Minute® White or Brown Rice, uncooked
1 package (5 ounces) pepperoni slices
1 jar (14 ounces) pizza sauce
1½ cups (6 ounces) shredded mozzarella cheese, divided
1 can (2.25 ounces) sliced black olives, drained (optional)

Prepare rice according to package directions. Combine rice, pepperoni, sauce, 1 cup cheese and olives, if desired, in large skillet over medium heat. Cook and stir until thoroughly heated. Top with remaining cheese before serving.

Serves 4

Tip:

Add mushrooms, green olives, sausage or Canadian bacon. (If using fresh mushrooms, cook and stir in hot skillet before adding rice and remaining ingredients.)

Rice, Broccoli 'n Cheese Cups

1 cup Minute® White Rice, uncooked
1 cup chicken broth
1 package (10 ounces) frozen chopped
      broccoli, thawed, drained*
1 cup shredded Cheddar cheese
¼ cup ranch dressing
2 eggs, lightly beaten

Or substitute 1 cup fresh chopped broccoli, cooked.

Preheat oven to 350°F. Prepare rice according to package directions, substituting chicken broth for water. Place cooked rice in large mixing bowl; cool slightly. Stir in remaining ingredients until well blended. Spoon mixture evenly into 8 greased muffin cups. Bake 20 minutes or until lightly browned.

Serves 8

Tip:

For party appetizers, use greased mini muffin tins and bake 10 to 12 minutes or until lightly browned.

Tutti Fruiti Rice Cream

1 cup Minute® White Rice, uncooked
1 can (15 ounces) tropical fruit salad, drained
2 cups miniature marshmallows
¼ cup sugar
1½ cups frozen nondairy whipped topping, thawed
Ground cinnamon (optional)

Prepare rice according to package directions. Cool. Toss with remaining ingredients. Chill. Sprinkle with cinnamon before serving, if desired.

Serves 4

Tip:

To sneak some whole-grain nutrition into your kids' diet, try substituting Minute® Brown Rice in dessert recipes. The flavor and texture will be just as appealing, and you'll feel even better about providing a second helping.

Warm Chocolate Risotto

- 1 cup Minute® White Rice, uncooked
- 1 cup milk
- ⅓ cup sugar
- 2 tablespoons unsalted butter
- ¼ cup heavy cream
- ½ cup semisweet chocolate chips
- Fresh mint leaves (optional)

Combine rice, milk and sugar in medium saucepan.
Bring to a boil. Remove from heat, cover and let stand
5 minutes. Stir in butter, cream and chocolate chips
until melted. Garnish with mint leaves, if desired.

Serves 4

Whole Grain Rice Pudding

1 cup Minute® Brown Rice, uncooked
1½ cups milk
⅓ cup maple syrup or honey
1 tablespoon butter
½ teaspoon ground cinnamon, nutmeg or allspice
Fresh mint leaves (optional)

Prepare rice according to package directions. Combine rice, milk, and maple syrup in medium saucepan. Bring to a boil; reduce heat and simmer 20 minutes, stirring frequently. Remove from heat, and stir in butter and cinnamon. Garnish with additional cinnamon and mint leaves, if desired.

Serves 4

Classic Minute Rice Pudding

3 cups milk
1 cup Minute® White Rice, uncooked
¼ cup sugar
¼ cup raisins
¼ teaspoon salt
2 large eggs
1 teaspoon vanilla

Combine milk, rice, sugar, raisins and salt in medium saucepan. Bring to a boil, stirring constantly. Reduce heat to medium-low; simmer 6 minutes, stirring occasionally. Beat eggs and vanilla lightly in a small bowl. Stir small amount of hot mixture into eggs. Stirring constantly, slowly pour egg mixture back into hot mixture. Stirring constantly, cook on low heat 1 minute until thickened. DO NOT BOIL. Remove from heat. Let stand 30 minutes. Serve warm. Store any remaining pudding in refrigerator.

Serves 4

Tip:

Create flavorful new varieties of rice puddings by trying different types of dried fruits, such as dried cherries, chopped dried apricots, chopped dried pineapple or dried sweetened cranberries.

Apple Cinnamon Rice Crisp

1 cup Minute® White or Brown Rice, uncooked
   Nonstick cooking spray
1 can (20 ounces) apple pie filling
1 cup packed brown sugar, divided
1 teaspoon ground cinnamon
½ cup raisins
½ cup walnuts, chopped
1½ cups uncooked rolled oats
4 tablespoons margarine
   Vanilla ice cream (optional)

Prepare rice according to package directions. Preheat oven to 350°F. Spray 2-quart baking dish with nonstick cooking spray. Combine rice, pie filling, ½ cup brown sugar, cinnamon, raisins and walnuts in medium bowl. Pour into prepared dish. In same bowl, combine remaining ½ cup brown sugar and rolled oats. Cut in margarine with pastry blender or fork, mixing well until mixture is moist. Sprinkle over rice mixture. Bake 20 minutes. Serve with ice cream, if desired.

Serves 8

Cherry Rice Cheesecake

2 cups Minute® White Rice, uncooked
Nonstick cooking spray
1 package (8 ounces)
    fat-free cream
    cheese, softened
1½ cups sugar, divided
1 cup fat-free sour
    cream
2 teaspoons vanilla
5 egg whites
2 tablespoons cornstarch*
1 can (15 ounces) sour red cherries,* undrained
1 tablespoon lemon juice*
Fresh mint leaves (optional)

Or omit remaining ½ cup sugar, cornstarch, sour red cherries and lemon juice; top cooled cheesecake with 1 can prepared cherry pie filling.

Prepare rice according to package directions. Preheat oven to 325°F. Lightly coat 9-inch springform pan with nonstick cooking spray; set aside. Combine cream cheese and 1 cup sugar in large bowl; beat until creamy. Stir in sour cream and vanilla. Add rice; mix well. In separate bowl, beat egg whites until soft peaks form. Fold into rice mixture. Pour into prepared pan. Bake 40 to 50 minutes or until set. Cool. While cheesecake is baking, combine remaining ½ cup sugar and cornstarch in small saucepan. Drain cherries, reserving liquid. Add reserved liquid to saucepan; mix well. Bring to a boil, stirring occasionally; simmer 1 minute or until thickened. Stir in cherries and lemon juice. Cool. Spoon over cheesecake. Garnish with mint leaves, if desired.

Serves 8